This Book Belongs to

....

....

The Planet Charleebob Explorer Notes

Borks

These docile creatures roam the plains of Charleebob, munching moss and pooping out balls of fragrant rainbow-coloured dung.

dung

fig 1.

Slender relative of the Ju-Ju-Bong Tree who occasionally visits at weekends.

Whipple Tree

Charleebob

A faraway planet, quite like our own Earth.

Scrambling Gawp

always looking

Half-plant, half-animal, and completely ridiculous, Gawps are able to run away from predators on their leg-like roots.

Frickle

The most intelligent animals on Charleebob and the only ones capable of throwing a decent party.

likes to build

legs

Innocuous Dill

(NOT to be confused with the Injurious Dollop) Jelly-like creature commonly found quivering in and around Charleebob's streams.

long tongue

Bezzler

fig 1.

Half-witted and always hungry, a Bezzler's favourite food is Frickles, but it will eat anything it can stuff into its grubby little mouth.

fig 2.

fuzzy

fig 3.

fig 1.

Ju-Ju *juicy* Bong Tree

The Ju-Ju-Bong's juicy leaves are a cool refreshing snack for thirsty animals.

6.

Enigmatic Desmond

um yum

Quinch

fig 1.

Crest

fig 2.

fig 3.

Hapicriss Moss

he Borks' main food, is bright yellow ant forms an edible arpet that covers most Charleebob's surface.

These playful bird-like creatures spend their days guzzling Ju-Ju-Bong juice and their nights getting up to go to the toilet.

For Charles Darwin, for explaining *how we all became* – JE

For ducks, llamas, centipedes, giant clams, pterodactyls and moles,
along with all the other funny-looking creatures
that helped me illustrate this book – ED

Text copyright © Jonathan Emmett 2018
Illustrations copyright © Elys Dolan 2018

First published in Great Britain and in the USA in 2018 by
Otter-Barry Books, Little Orchard, Burley Gate, Herefordshire, HR1 3QS
www.otterbarrybooks.com

This paperback edition first published in Great Britain in 2019

A catalogue record for this book is available from the British Library.

ISBN 978-1-910959-66-4

Illustrated with watercolour

Printed in China

1 3 5 7 9 8 6 4 2

How the BORKs BECAME

Words by **Jonathan Emmett**

Pictures by **Elys Dolan**

Otter-Barry BOOKS

On a faraway planet, quite like our own Earth,
a bunch of Bork mothers has just given birth

to a great brood of Borklings, in all shapes and sizes.
Some look like their parents – but some are surprises.

The thing about Borks is, no two are a match.
They're **all** a bit different, just look at this batch.

These odd little differences help the Borks thrive.
Without them, it's doubtful they'd still be alive.

You see, Borks haven't **always** looked as they do.
Their fur was once short and its colour was blue,
and those long, skinny necks that make them so tall
were once very squat and not skinny at all.

This might start you wondering, wondering **HOW?**

How did the Borks become what they are now?

What caused all these changes? What brought them about?

Well, we'll have to go back a few years to find out....

On a faraway planet, quite like our own Earth,
a bunch of Bork mothers had just given birth
to a great brood of Borklings, in all shapes and sizes.
Some looked like their parents – but some were surprises.

While most of the Borklings had fur that was short,
there were also a few of a shaggier sort.
These shaggy-furred Borklings, they looked kind of funny
and got rather hot when the weather was sunny.

But later that year, when the weather turned chilly,
the shaggy-furred Borks did not feel quite so silly.

While the shorter-furred Borks couldn't cope with the storm,
their shaggy-furred cousins kept perfectly warm.

And when the storm stopped and a new day arrived,
only the shaggy-furred Borks had survived!

So the next time a big Borkling birthing occurred,
all of the babies were born shaggy-furred.
While most of these offspring were bright shades of blue,
some were bright yellow, but only a few.

These bright yellow Borklings looked rather bizarre
and weren't very easy to spot from afar,
as their fur blended in with the bright yellow moss
which covered the plain that the Borks roamed across.

SNIFF!

They were roaming this plain on a hot sunny day
when a **Ravenous Snarfle** came flying their way.

Now there's nothing a Snarfle likes more for its lunch than a beakful of Borks . . .

so it snatched up a bunch!
It gobbled up every last Bork it could find,
every last one – but it left some behind.

The big beastly bird would have gobbled the lot,
but the bright yellow Borks had been too hard to spot.

And so, when the next batch of babies came through,
all of the offspring were yellow, not blue.

But, while most of these Borklings had necks that were squat,
there were also a few who had necks that were not!
These skinny-necked Borklings looked rather absurd,
with their heads towering over the rest of the herd.

But later that year, when the weather grew dry,
these tall Borks were glad to have heads up so high.
For without any rain the moss shrivelled up dead,
and moss was the food on which every Bork fed.

So with nothing to eat, many Borks died off too,
almost all of the herd, except for a few.

For the skinny-necked Borks things were not quite so dire,
because, thanks to those necks, they could reach a bit higher
and feed on the branches of Ju-Ju-Bong trees,
which held lots of water within their thick leaves.

So we're back where we started, but now you know **HOW**.
You know how the Borks became what they are now.

And if anyone asks how this mystery is solved,
you can tell them the answer – they simply **EVOLVED!**

It's truly remarkable, wondrous and strange,
how through **EVOLUTION** a creature can change.

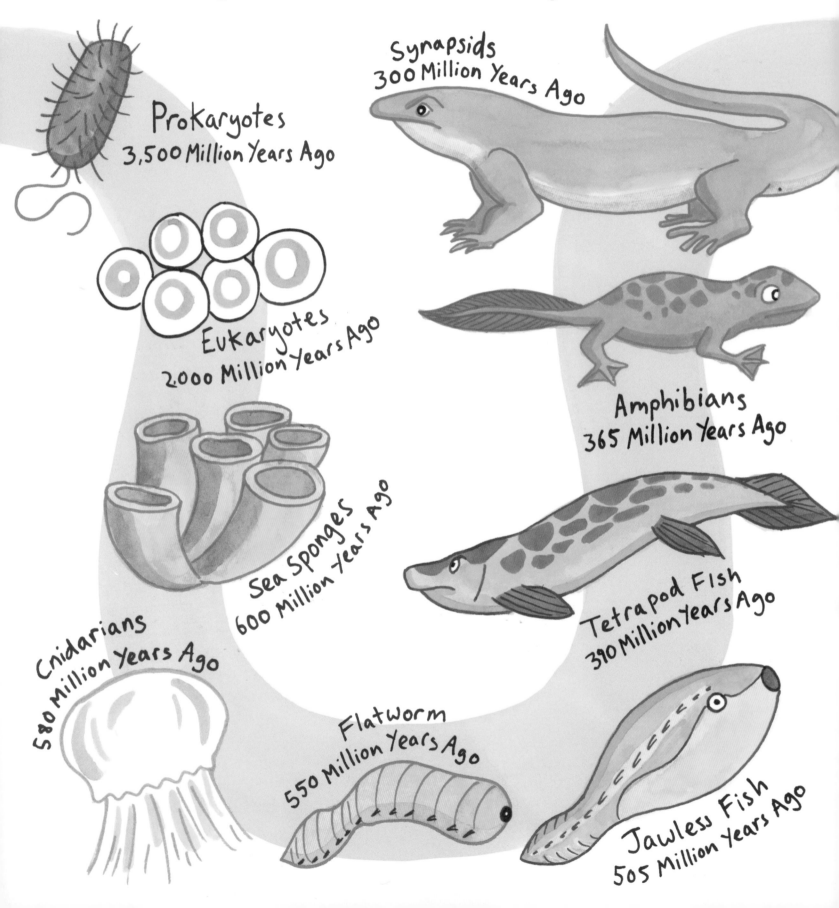

Prokaryotes
3,500 Million Years Ago

Synapsids
300 Million Years Ago

Eukaryotes
2000 Million Years Ago

Amphibians
365 Million Years Ago

Sea Sponges
600 Million Years Ago

Cnidarians
580 Million Years Ago

Tetrapod Fish
390 Million Years Ago

Flatworm
550 Million Years Ago

Jawless Fish
505 Million Years Ago

Evolution explains many other things too.
It even explains just how **YOU** became **YOU!**

YOU!

Mammals
220 Million Years Ago

Homo Heidelbergensis
0.5 Million Years Ago

Proto-Primates
65 Million Years Ago

Homo Sapiens
0.2 Million Years Ago

Homo Habilis
2.5 Million Years Ago

Darwinius
47 Million Years Ago

Proconsul
27 Million Years Ago

Sahelanthropus
Tchadensis
7 Million Years Ago

EVOLUTION ON EARTH

Evolution is a scientific theory that explains how animals and plants can gradually change over time. Evolution happens very quickly on the Borks' planet and there are big changes each time the Borks have babies.

For Earth animals, the changes are usually much smaller and not so easy to spot. Because Earth animals only change a tiny bit at a time, they take much longer to evolve. It might take an Earth animal millions of years to change as much as the Borks in the story do.

Charles Darwin,
the English scientist who published
his theory of evolution,
On the Origin of Species, in 1859.

Charles Darwin came up with his
theory of evolution after visiting
the Galapagos Islands
in South America.

Spotted Slunky

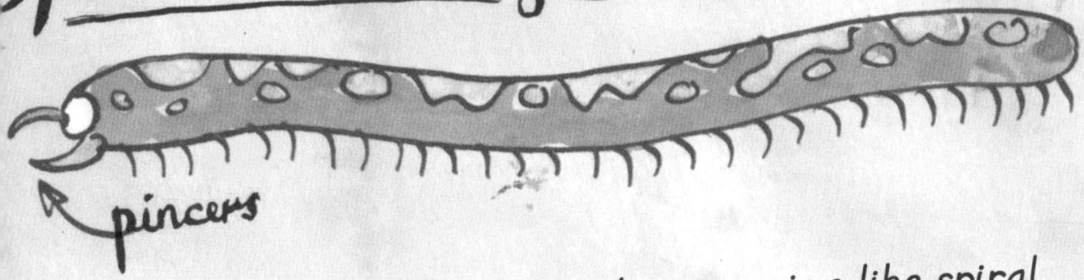

fig 1.

pincers

This many-legged predator has a spring-like spiral skeleton that allows it to launch itself into the air.

Voracious Champ

This snappy flesh-eating plant produces a sweet, marmalade-like nectar to lure unwary creatures.

fig 1.   fig 2   fig 3

Scootle

Small and incredibly adaptable, the Scootle is like a living Swiss Army knife.

Slaying Mantis

antenna

Sly and stealthy Scootle-scoffing predator, also known as a Fugwinkle.

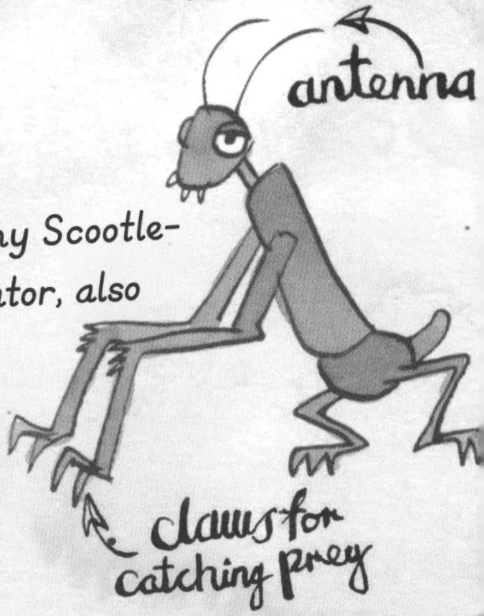

claws for catching prey

Ravenous Snarfle

brightly coloured plumage

mean

Crest

many eyes

The largest predator on Charleebob, the Snarfle cruises the skies like a huge, sinister, Bork-gobbling jumbo jet.

long

fig 1.

About the Author
and Illustrator

Jonathan Emmett was born in Leicestershire.
He trained and worked as an architect but left the profession
to become a stay-at-home dad and pursue a career as an
author and paper engineer. Now Jonathan is an award-winning
writer who has had more than 60 books published, including
*Bringing Down the Moon, Someone Bigger, The Princess and
the Pig, Pigs Might Fly* and *The Pig's Knickers*, and his work has
been translated into over 30 different languages. He lives
in Nottingham with his wife and two children.

www.scribblestreet.co.uk

• • •

Elys Dolan is a writer and illustrator who makes books
about everything from seagull detectives, capitalist bunny
rabbits and weasels plotting world domination to
German goats and marauding doughnuts. Her bestselling
picture books include *Weasels, Steven Seagull Action Hero* and
The Doughnut of Doom. She works predominantly with ink,
new-fangled digital witchcraft and coloured pencils.
Elys is a lecturer on the MA in Children's Book Illustration
at the Cambridge School of Art. She lives in Cambridge.

www.elysdolan.com